How to Manifest Wealth

A Human's Journey to Prosperity in 2023

Chapter 1

Laying the Foundation

Building wealth is much like building a house. Before we can start constructing walls or install windows, we need to lay a solid foundation. Similarly, your journey to riches begins with establishing a robust base. This base is not just about money. It's about cultivating a mindset of abundance, discipline, and persistence.

1.1 Cultivating an Abundance Mindset

An abundance mindset is about believing that there's plenty out there for everyone. It's about realizing that money is not a zero-sum game where the rich get richer at the expense of the poor. There are countless opportunities and resources in the world that are waiting to be tapped into. By developing an abundance mindset, we encourage a positive relationship with money, viewing it as a tool to help us achieve our goals rather than a limited resource that induces stress and fear.

1.2 Discipline is Key

Discipline is a non-negotiable attribute of wealth creation. It involves taking consistent actions towards our goals, regardless of how we're feeling. It could be something as simple as saving a portion of your income each month or spending a few hours each week learning about investment strategies. The key here is consistency. It might not feel like you're making significant progress in the short term, but remember, we're building wealth over a lifetime.

1.3 Persistence Pays Off

There will be roadblocks on your journey to wealth. You might lose money on an investment, or an unexpected expense might come up that drains your savings. This is where persistence comes in. Persistence is about having the determination to keep going despite setbacks. It's about believing in your capacity to overcome challenges and learning from your mistakes rather than letting them defeat you.

1.4 Visualize Your Success

Finally, to set the right foundation, visualize your success. Imagine yourself living the life you want, having achieved your financial goals. What does it feel like? What are you doing? Who are you with? Visualization not only helps cement your goals in your mind, but it also motivates you to take actions towards achieving them.

This first step towards building wealth might not involve a single dollar, but it's crucial. Your mindset, discipline, persistence, and the clarity of your vision are the cornerstones of your financial journey. Cultivate them, and you'll be well-prepared to embark on this exciting journey to prosperity.

Chapter 2

Taking the Financial Wheel

Embarking on your journey to wealth is a thrilling adventure. Like any epic journey, it begins by understanding where you are. In financial terms, this means getting to know your income, your expenses, and your debts intimately. It might not be the most exciting first step, but it's a crucial one.

2.1 Income: More than Just a Paycheck

The word 'income' often brings to mind images of monthly paychecks. But it's so much more than that. Think about your income as a river. Your salary might be the mainstream, but there could be other smaller streams flowing into it. These could be anything from bonuses at work, to that Etsy shop you started during lockdown, to the dividends from that stock your grandpa gave you. It's essential to account for every stream, no matter how small. The broader your river, the greater your potential to save and invest.

2.2 Expenses: The Necessary (and Unnecessary) Evils

We all have expenses - those unavoidable costs of living that sometimes seem to suck our wallets dry. But when you break down your expenses into clear categories - fixed essentials like rent or utilities, variable essentials like groceries, and non-essentials like nights out or Netflix subscriptions - you suddenly have a clearer picture. You might even identify some areas where your money seems to disappear needlessly. Spoiler alert: You probably don't need to be subscribed to five different streaming platforms.

2.3 Net Worth: The Big Picture

Knowing your net worth is like standing on a hill overlooking your financial landscape. Your net worth is your assets (everything you own of value) minus your liabilities (everything you owe). This number might not look impressive right now, but that's okay. The important part is watching it grow over time. You'll climb higher up that hill and get a better view as you continue on your journey.

2.4 Budgeting: It's Not a Dirty Word

Budgeting gets a bad rap. Many view it as a kind of financial diet, restricting your spending and sucking the joy out of life. But it's not about deprivation. It's about understanding how your money flows and steering it in the right direction. Your budget is your roadmap, guiding your spending choices and helping you navigate towards your financial goals.

2.5 Debts: Conquer Your Financial Foes

Debt is the villain in our wealth-building story. It's the dragon hoarding our treasure or the highwayman demanding our hard-earned coin. It's crucial to understand your debts, especially those with high interest rates like credit cards. Prioritize slaying these beasts, but remember to stash some gold in your treasure chest (i.e., savings) along the way.

Understanding your financial position might not be glamorous. But remember, every hero's journey starts somewhere, often in the humblest of places. It's not about where you are now, but where you're going. Buckle up and enjoy the ride.

Chapter 3

The Magic of Regular Savings

In the world of wealth creation, one often overlooks the humble act of saving. It's not as sexy as investing in a fast-growing startup or as exciting as flipping a house for profit, but saving money is the silent hero on your journey to riches. It's like the tortoise in the age-old fable, slowly but surely making its way to the finish line.

3.1 Understanding the Power of Saving

The idea of saving isn't new or revolutionary. As kids, many of us had piggy banks where we'd stash away coins. Yet, as we grow older, the act of saving often becomes more complex. Suddenly, there are bills to pay, emergencies to cater to, and those irresistible sales that make us whip out our credit cards. The simple act of setting money aside becomes a challenge.

Saving money isn't about denying yourself the pleasures of life. Rather, it's about postponing immediate gratification for long-term security and wealth.

3.2 The Habit of Saving

Creating a habit of saving is like building a muscle. It might be difficult at first, but over time it gets stronger, and the process becomes easier. Start with small, achievable targets. Saving just a little bit consistently can make a big difference in the long run.

It can be as simple as committing to save 10% of your monthly income. Over time, you may be surprised at how this sum can grow, and you'll likely find ways to increase the percentage you save.

3.3 Emergency Funds: Your Financial Safety Net

The unexpected happens. Cars break down. Medical emergencies occur. Jobs can be lost. These events can be stressful, but having a financial safety net can help. That's the role of an emergency fund.

This is a stash of money set aside to cover financial surprises life throws your way. It's generally recommended to have 3-6 months' worth of living expenses in your emergency fund. You hope you'll never have to use it, but it's there if you need it, offering peace of mind.

3.4 Long-Term Savings: Your Future Self Will Thank You

As you add to your savings, consider thinking long term. Saving for retirement might seem far away at first glance, but the sooner you start saving the more time your money has to grow.

Every little bit you save now can mean a more comfortable and secure retirement. Plus, it's always a good feeling knowing you're working towards a future where you can kick back and relax.

The act of saving may seem slow and unglamorous. But remember, it's the tortoise that won the race. Adopting a saver's mindset, creating good saving habits, and having clear saving goals can set you on the path to financial abundance.

Chapter 4

Navigating the Investment Landscape

Imagine you're an explorer. You've traveled through the land of income, braved the swamps of expenses, and climbed the mountain of saving. Now, you stand before the vast landscape of investing. It's unknown territory, full of potential rewards and lurking risks. But don't worry, you're prepared, and you're ready for the adventure.

4.1 Investing: What is it Really?

Many see investing as an elusive, complicated concept, the playground of Wall Street tycoons and financial wizards. But strip away the jargon, and it's pretty simple. Investing is about putting your money to work for you, letting it grow and multiply over time. Think of it as your money going off on its own little adventures, returning home with more than it left with.

4.2 Understanding Risk and Reward

Investing is not without its risks. Like any adventure, there are chances of loss and danger. However, every risk also carries a potential reward. The trick is to balance the two, taking calculated risks where the potential rewards outweigh the possible losses. Don't be afraid of risk, but respect it.

4.3 The Magic of Compound Interest

Remember our friend, the tortoise? It's back, but this time, it's brought a magic trick— compound interest. Albert Einstein famously called compound interest the eighth wonder of the world. It's the snowball effect of your investments, where the returns you earn start earning their own returns. It might not seem like much at first, but give it time, and you'll be amazed at the results.

4.4 Diversify Your Portfolio: Don't Put All Your Eggs in One Basket

As the saying goes, don't put all your eggs in one basket. Spreading your investments across a variety of assets (like stocks, bonds, real estate, etc.) can help manage risk. If one investment performs poorly, others may perform well. It's all about balance.

4.5 Consistency is Key

Remember, investing is not a get-rich-quick scheme. It's a long-term game. Consistency is key. Regular investments, no matter how small, can accumulate over time, thanks to our friend, compound interest.

The realm of investing may seem intimidating, but don't let that deter you. With knowledge, patience, and a dash of courage, you can navigate this landscape successfully. Remember, every great explorer started with their first step. Your investment journey is just beginning, and it's going to be an exciting ride.

Chapter 5

Your Financial Allies - Taxes and Insurance

As you traverse the terrain of financial abundance, there are two companions often perceived as foes: taxes and insurance. However, when approached with understanding and strategy, these seemingly challenging components of your financial journey can become powerful allies.

5.1 Taxes: Turning the 'Burden' into a Benefit

Taxes often evoke feelings of dread and frustration. But, like it or not, taxes are a part of life. The key is to understand them and learn how to navigate the tax system effectively.

For instance, many governments offer tax advantages for certain activities, such as investing in retirement accounts, education expenses, or health insurance. By understanding these incentives, you can maximize your income and savings.

5.2 Insurance: Protecting Your Wealth

While accumulating wealth is important, protecting it is just as crucial. Life can throw unexpected curveballs at us - illness, accidents, property damage. These unexpected events can quickly drain our savings. This is where insurance comes in.

Different types of insurance provide protection for various aspects of our lives. Health insurance for medical expenses, homeowner's insurance for property damage, life insurance for family support after death, disability insurance for income protection in case of disability, and the list goes on.

The right insurance policy can serve as a shield, protecting your wealth from life's unexpected events.

5.3 Incorporating Taxes and Insurance into Your Financial Plan

Tax planning and insurance aren't standalone activities but should be integral parts of your overall financial plan. By understanding and effectively using tax laws, you can keep more of your hard-earned money. By selecting the right insurance policies, you can protect your wealth and provide for a secure future.

At first glance, taxes and insurance might seem like formidable obstacles in your quest to build wealth. Yet when explored more thoroughly, they can actually serve as allies in safeguarding and expanding your portfolio - it all boils down to having knowledge and strategic planning skills.

Chapter 6

Building Multiple Streams of Income

Imagine you're on a journey down a river toward the ocean of wealth. Would you rather rely on one stream to get there or have multiple tributaries pushing you forward? As you navigate your way toward financial abundance, establishing multiple streams of income can accelerate your journey and offer added security.

6.1 The Importance of Multiple Income Streams

Relying on a single source of income is a bit like standing on one leg - it works, but it's a shaky foundation. The loss of that income can significantly impact your financial stability. Multiple income streams offer a safety net and a diversified income can make the journey toward wealth more stable and quicker.

6.2 Active Income: Trading Time for Money

Active income is where you trade your time and effort for money. This includes your job or any side gig that requires active participation. While there's a limit to the amount of work you can do and thus money you can earn, active income is a reliable stream that can fund your lifestyle and your investments.

6.3 Passive Income: Let Your Money Work For You

Passive income is money earned with minimal activity through a variety of ventures which require an initial start-up effort or initial financial investment but then they continue to generate income over time. This could be income from a rental property, royalties from a book you wrote, or dividends from your investments. The beauty of passive income is that it can provide income without your active involvement, giving you more time and freedom.

6.4 Semi-Passive Income: A Middle Ground

Semi-passive income is a blend of active and passive income. It requires some initial effort, but once set up, it demands less time to maintain. Examples might include an online course you create or a small business you start.

6.5 Exploring Your Income Options

The options for creating additional income streams are plentiful, limited only by your interests, skills, and willingness to put in the effort. You might rent out a room in your house, start a blog, or invest in stocks. The key is to find something that aligns with your lifestyle, skills, and financial goals.

Creating multiple income streams may require more effort and investment upfront, but the rewards can be substantial. Not only does it provide financial stability, but it also brings you closer to financial independence, where you're no longer solely reliant on your job for income. That's a powerful place to be.

Chapter 7

Staying the Course: The Power of Persistence and Patience

You've built your boat, gathered your provisions, and set sail on the sea of financial abundance. You've discovered how to navigate the currents of income, savings, and investment. You've learned to respect the storms of tax and insurance, and you've harnessed the winds of multiple income streams. Now comes the test of endurance. It's time to stay the course.

7.1 Understanding the Long Game

Building wealth isn't a sprint; it's a marathon. It requires consistent effort, strategic planning, and most importantly, patience. As in a marathon, you may face challenges or obstacles that slow you down. There may be times when your progress feels painfully slow, but remember, the race is not always to the swift but to those who keep on running.

7.2 Dealing with Financial Setbacks

Life doesn't always go according to plan. You might face unexpected expenses, lose a job, or experience investment losses. These financial setbacks can be discouraging, but remember, they're just part of the journey. They are not the end but learning opportunities. They can teach us to plan better, to save more, or to diversify our income sources.

7.3 Celebrating Small Victories

On your journey, don't forget to celebrate the small victories. Each time you pay off a debt, reach a saving goal, or earn from an investment, take a moment to acknowledge your progress. These small wins keep us motivated and remind us that we're moving in the right direction.

7.4 The Power of Persistence

The road to wealth requires persistence. There will be times when your goals seem out of reach, when your efforts seem in vain, but remember, persistence pays off. Just as the Grand Canyon was formed by persistent water erosion, so too can your wealth grow with persistent effort.

7.5 Never Stop Learning

The financial world is always changing. New investment opportunities arise, tax laws change, and global events can impact the economy. To stay ahead, commit to lifelong learning. Read books, follow financial news, or even take a course. Knowledge is power, and in the financial world, it can equate to dollars.

Remaining focused and staying the course can be difficult, yet essential to reaching wealth. Remember that each journey starts with one step and becomes composed of thousands more - not about speed but endurance, patience, and persistence! Keep going until you reach your destination.

Chapter 8

The Art of Giving: Philanthropy and Financial Abundance

As you reach the advanced stages of your wealth journey, a new horizon emerges: the art of giving back. As counterintuitive as it may seem, giving is a key component of financial abundance. By learning how to give wisely, you're not only enhancing your personal growth but also making a significant impact in the world.

8.1 Understanding Philanthropy

Philanthropy derives its name from the Greek term, "philanthropia," meaning "love of humanity." Philanthropy goes beyond simply writing checks to charity organizations; it involves harnessing your resources - money, time or skills - in order to make an impactful change for good in this world.

8.2 The Benefits of Giving

Giving does more than just help others. It also comes with personal benefits. Numerous studies have found that giving can lead to greater happiness, health, and a sense of purpose in life. Plus, many countries offer tax benefits for charitable donations, meaning you can support causes you care about while also reducing your tax bill.

8.3 How to Give Wisely

There's no one-size-fits-all approach to philanthropy. However, here are some tips to give wisely:

- Research: Before you donate, do your homework. Ensure the organization you're supporting is reputable and uses donations effectively.
- Align with Your Values: Choose causes that resonate with your personal values and passions.
- Plan Your Giving: Like any financial decision, giving should be planned. Decide how much you can afford to give and budget for it.

8.4 The Power of Impact Investing

Another way to contribute positively is through impact investing. This involves investing in companies, organizations, and funds with the intention to generate a measurable, beneficial social or environmental impact alongside a financial return.

8.5 Leaving a Legacy

Philanthropy can also be a part of your legacy. By setting up trusts, foundations, or bequests in your will, you can continue to make a positive impact long after you're gone.

At its core, wealth is about more than just money. It's about creating a life of abundance, not just for ourselves but for those around us. As you journey toward financial abundance, remember the art of giving back. It's a testament to your success and a powerful way to make a difference in the world.

Chapter 9

Lifelong Learning and Adaptability: The Unseen Wealth

We've journeyed together through the terrain of personal finance, understanding income, mastering expenses, appreciating savings, exploring investments, respecting taxes and insurance, and realizing the power of multiple income streams. We've learned the importance of perseverance and the joy of giving. Now, as we near the end of our journey, we focus on two key elements that often go unnoticed: lifelong learning and adaptability.

9.1 Embrace Lifelong Learning

In our rapidly changing world, being open to new ideas and continually learning is vital for sustained financial growth. From the shifting landscapes of the stock market to the rise of cryptocurrency, the financial world is continually evolving. Staying informed about these changes allows you to make informed decisions and seize new opportunities.

Read books, take courses, listen to podcasts, or seek a mentor. Never stop filling your mind with new knowledge and insights.

9.2 The Power of Adaptability

As is often said, change is the only constant in life. Your circumstances, economic climate and goals all change over time - what separates successful people is their ability to adapt with these shifts in a timely manner.

When faced with change, view it not as a threat, but as an opportunity for growth. Just as a ship adjusts its sails to the changing wind, learn to adapt your financial strategies to the changing circumstances.

9.3 Building Your Financial Intelligence

Lifelong learning and adaptability both contribute to what's known as financial intelligence. This goes beyond understanding numbers; financial intelligence means making smart financial decisions, mitigating risks, capitalizing on opportunities and remaining resilient when confronted by financial setbacks.

9.4 From Financial Literacy to Financial Wisdom

As you continue learning and adapting, you evolve from being financially literate to being financially wise. Financial literacy means you understand the basics of personal finance. Financial wisdom, on the other hand, means you know how to apply this knowledge to make sound financial decisions.

The journey toward financial abundance is not just about accumulating wealth, but also about cultivating your financial intelligence and wisdom. Embrace lifelong learning, be adaptable, and continue evolving your financial strategies. After all, true wealth lies not just in your bank account, but also in the richness of your knowledge and the flexibility of your approach.

Chapter 10

The Journey Ahead: Your Path to Financial Abundance

You've navigated the landscape of personal finance, scaled its mountains, crossed its rivers, and found your way through its forests. Now, you stand on the brink of your journey ahead, equipped with the knowledge and strategies you need to build your wealth. This final chapter isn't an ending, but a beginning - the start of your path to financial abundance.

10.1 Recap of the Journey

Together, we've covered much ground. We explored the importance of understanding your income and expenses in order to manage them, the power of savings, the benefits of investments, and diversifying income sources. Furthermore, we discovered how taxes and insurance can actually become allies rather than enemies, the significance of perseverance, and the transformative potential of giving - not forgetting how continuous learning and adaptability play such an essential role in building wealth.

10.2 The Wealth Mindset

A crucial lesson to remember is that building wealth begins in the mind. Your beliefs about money, your financial habits, your ability to set and pursue goals, and your willingness to take calculated risks - these all form your wealth mindset. Cultivate a mindset of abundance, resilience, and determination.

10.3 Your Personal Financial Plan

Now is the time to put this knowledge into action by developing your personal financial plan. Your plan should reflect your financial goals, current status and long-term ambitions; and serve as a road map on your journey toward wealth accumulation.

10.4 Remember: It's a Marathon, Not a Sprint

Building wealth is a long-term endeavor. It requires patience, persistence, and a lot of hard work. But remember, the journey itself can be as rewarding as the destination. Celebrate your milestones, learn from your setbacks, and never stop striving for your goals.

10.5 Onward to Financial Abundance

You're now armed with the knowledge and strategies you need to build financial abundance. But remember, the world of personal finance is always evolving. Stay curious, continue learning, and remain adaptable. Your journey to wealth is just beginning, and the path ahead is filled with potential.

Thank you for joining me on this journey. Here's to your financial success, to the wealth you will build, and to the abundant life you will create. Onward, to your financial future!

Conclusion

Embrace Your Journey to Financial Abundance

We began our journey together exploring the landscape of personal finance, and now we stand on the precipice of your individual financial journey. It's a journey that will be marked by triumphs and setbacks, moments of clarity, and periods of confusion. But as with all great journeys, the real reward is in the journey itself.

The knowledge and tools you've gained from this book are meant to guide you, but your path will be uniquely your own. As you make decisions, remember the core principles we discussed - the power of saving, the importance of investment, the security of diversified income, the necessary allies of tax and insurance, the unyielding value of persistence, and the beauty of giving. Above all, remember the transformative power of continuous learning and adaptability.

Building wealth is about more than just accumulating money. It's about cultivating a rich life - a life filled with purpose, joy, and financial freedom. It's about taking control of your financial destiny and shaping it to fit your dreams and goals.

As you embark on your journey toward financial abundance, keep in mind that the road to wealth is not a straight line. It will require effort, resilience, and a commitment to lifelong learning. But with every step you take, every decision you make, you're not just building wealth; you're building the life you desire.

Remember, wealth is not the destination but the journey. It's the process of striving, growing, and learning. It's about becoming the best version of yourself and creating a life of abundance.

Thank you for joining me on this journey. Here's to your financial success, to the wealth you will build, and to the life of abundance that lies ahead. Onward to your financial future! Let the journey continue!